Anna M. Morrison Reed

The Later Poems of Anna M. Morrison

Anna M. Morrison Reed

The Later Poems of Anna M. Morrison

ISBN/EAN: 9783744651943

Printed in Europe, USA, Canada, Australia, Japan

Cover: Foto ©Thomas Meinert / pixelio.de

More available books at **www.hansebooks.com**

THE'

LATER POEMS

OF

ANNA MORRISON REED

- - --

IN ONE VOLUME

SAN FRANCISCO
J. STUART & COMPANY, PUBLISHERS
1891

PRINTED BY P. M. DIERS & CO., SAN FRANCISCO.

TO THE MEMORY OF MY MOTHER.

CONTENTS

—

THE LATER POEMS

· · OF · ·

ANNA MORRISON REED

Her King

A WINSOME maiden planned her life—
  How, where she was her hero's wife,
He should be royal among men,
And worthy of a diadem.
Through all the devious ways of earth
  She sought her king;
The snows of Winter fell before—
  She walked o'er flowers of vanished Spring;
Into the Summer's fragrant heat
She bent her quest, with rapid feet,
Then saddened; still she journeyed down
The Autumn hillsides, bare and brown,
Through shadowy eves and golden morns;
And lo she found him—crowned with thorns.

Death of President Garfield

A MONODY

READ IN UKIAH, CALIFORNIA, MONDAY, SEPTEMBER 26TH, 1881.

(From the Ukiah Dispatch and Democrat.)

MRS. ANNA M. REED then stepped to the front and read the following eloquent and most beautiful monody on the death of him who has gone from earth's scenes of toil and trouble to the realms of everlasting life, where "the wicked cease from troubling" and the "weary be at rest;" there where "the small and the great" are gathered. The reading was almost faultless, and the impression made was one of deep solemnity. The sentiments are those of a truly Christian heart, and the pathos therein contained awakened the tenderest emotions.

TOLL all the bells! a great soul's passed away
From clouds and shadows to the perfect day;
The wasted garment that is left behind
Must be to ashes and to dust consigned.
The tears of suffering death has wiped away,
But who shall dry the eyes of those who stay—
The aged mother and the faithful wife?
The children wailing for that ended life?
The nation calling for the leader slain,
Who long weeks languished on his bed of pain?
Toll all the bells, beat low the muffled drum;
In long procession mourning millions come
To honor him who, in a land of laws,
By lawless hand has died, without a cause.

Beside the ocean, that, with measured surge,
Chanted his first and grandest funeral dirge—
Sublimest minstrel at the feet of God;
It still sang on, while fell the mystic rod
And moaned a requiem for the parting soul,
Soaring beyond this little world's control.
No human voice may sing of him so well,
Nor all the grandeur of his history tell;
But to his memory, out of many lands,
Will struggling genius lift aspiring hands
To him who fortune's darkest frowns withstood,
And kept his every aim still great and good—
Who reached the summit of the hill of fame
With life unblemished and unsullied name—
A grand rebuke to every weaker heart
That tempted, turneth from the better part;
Reproaching those who, like the one of old,
Their birthright for a "mess of pottage" sold.
His mind, untrammeled, was as broad as Earth;
His heart was centered at his family hearth—
He made his home a type of all things seem
Of which the honest Christian soul can dream,
Fit emblem of that home in fairer lands
Where mansions wait, not built by human hands.

The annals of the past one truth repeat
Of those, whose lives with greatness were replete—
This fact, more eloquent than all beside,
Whate'er their history, they all have died.
Sceptre or crown, the pride of place or power
To frail mortality loaned but for an hour,
When death had pointed to the solemn bier,
They learned the mockery of all things here ;
Sowing that others might the harvest reap,
Along the wayside they have gone to sleep—
Tired of the treasures that the years may rust,
Tired of the things that are but sordid dust, [steal,
Tired of the gold that thieves break through and
Tired of the wrongs successive years reveal—
The graves of such, like landmarks, strew the sod,
Pointing submission to the will of God.

But though the souls of men like him we mourn
On waves of mystery are beyond us borne—
A grateful world their names perpetuate,
And well may strive their deeds to emulate ;
For though they drift beyond the tides of fame,
We feel, indeed, they have not lived in vain.
A proud inheritance has this one left

To all his loved ones and the land bereft—
His pure example may the world defy—
His glorious principles can never die;
Nor that so blessed and so heaven-sent,
On which its authors based our government,
Where earnest manhood, by its simple worth,
Depends not on the accident of birth—
By honest labor, without gold to buy,
May earn and reach its stations proud and high.

Oh! let the flags droop low—toll all the bells;
We lay him down amid our last farewells.
Under the earth, with loving tributes dressed,
Do we resign him to his lasting rest;
And to Columbia, still safe and free,
We trust the honor of his memory;
As turns his sacred clay to kindred sod,
His martyred spirit finds repose with God.

Mother--A Reverie

———

IN the brush fence by the lane
  I hear the stormbirds crying,
And I know the winter rain
    Soon will beat where thou art lying;
For the wind and rain are near,
    When the stormbirds are a-crying.
A brave, bright, winter rose
    Taps the window where I'm sitting;
Its heart with beauty glows,
    While the autumn hours are flitting;
It taps the silent pane
    Of the window where I'm sitting.
The south wind kisses light
    Its petals, curved and folded,
Like a picture warm and bright,
    Close in the heart enfolded—
Like a dream of love and youth,
    In the heart of age enfolded.
And it speaks to me of thee,
    While the stormbirds are a-crying,

Though thy face I cannot see,
  Thy memory is lying
In the winter of my heart,
  Best, brightest and undying.
I dream of thee so dear,
  Before the woodfire glowing;
I hear the herd-bells clear,
  And the cattle softly lowing;
The sounds foretell the rain,
  While the fire is brightly glowing.
In thought I pass the lane
  Where stormbirds are a-crying,
As to some sacred fane,
  To the grave where thou art lying,
Through fragrant pine-wood aisles
  Where the sunset glow is dying;
Where one can not hear the noise
  Of a footfall on the mosses;
Where the pine leaves lightly poise
  Like a pile of russet flosses;
Where the rabbit or the squirrel,
  With silent footstep, crosses;
Where the brake, with quiv'ring fronds,
  Beside the gravestone whispers

The earliest matin songs,
   And at eve the sadder vespers,
That the night wind softly taught
   The leaves to chant in whispers.
There so quietly you sleep,
   While the restless winds are sighing,
In the grave so dark and deep,
   Nor heed the stormbirds crying,
Nor the tears that fall like rain,
   And my heart within me dying.
The rose taps on the pane,
   And the stormbirds are a-crying,
And I soon will hear the rain
   Beat through the wind's low sighing,
While rose leaves flutter down
   On the grave where thou are lying.

Washington

1789-1889

ACROSS a century of change
  We reach our hands to thee—
Toward one bright and changeless thing,
  Thy honored memory.

Along the battlements of Time
  No hero lived and died
Whose name in song and deathless rhyme
  Is uttered with such pride.

It stirs the heart of free-born men,
  And whispers to the slave
The truths that e'en make eloquent
  The silence of thy grave.

No stain was on thy grand career
  Of lust, or pride or greed ;
Thy sword was never bared because
  Of some unhallowed creed.

O Washington! if from the realms
　　Of perfect love and light
The immortal thought of one like thee
　　May earthward take its flight,

Look down upon this land to-day—
　　Across from sea to sea—
Thy great soul will be thrilled to know
　　How much we honor thee.

We ask in thy dear name to be
　　Made faithful to our trust,
And lay our wreaths of immortelles
　　Upon thy sacred dust.

Wasted

NOT Time, that sacred heritage to all,
    For in the cycles that have passed away
I cannot count me one lost, idle day,
Nor opportunity; to fate's most meager gift,
I have been eager, heart and hand to lift.
What waste could then my faithful life befall?

A cheek whose roses bloomed for eyes so blind,
They did not see they were the rarest kind;
Words that the world had listened for for years,
Falling unanswered on the dullest ears;
A heart worn out—as fond as ever beat,
Its wine of life spilled at unworthy feet;
A soul so tortured, as years come and go,
Its wasted treasure, God alone can know.

Retrospect

___

THERE is a witching mem'ry my heart so oft
    recalls—
A silver cornet ringing above the palace walls,
Where from a draperied window a bright young
    face looked down
Upon my lady's garden that graced Yokaya's town.

Where passion flower and jasmine diffused a fra-
    grant balm;
Where shone the brilliant salvia and whispered
    pine and palm;
The willow o'er the fountain, with fingers long and
    slim,
Reached to the sparkling water that kissed the
    fretted brim,
And many a woodland songster, awearied with the
    heat,
Bathed in the cooling crystal and sang his matin
    sweet.

O days, whose dawn's pink splendor waxed to a
  golden noon!
O perfume, song and blossom, in life's impassioned
  rune!
O south wind, blowing gently the petals at my feet!
O twilight, stealing over! O kisses, rare and sweet!
O little maiden, singing beside the stately hall!
O silver cornet, ringing above the palace wall!

"Gertrude and Theodore"

A LAY OF YE MODERN KNIGHT AND LADY FAIR.

WITH a ring of hoofs I heard them pass,
  As the horses spurned the brittle grass;
A youth and maid of our modern time,
On the morning side of life's sweet prime.
Active and graceful, and fair and young
As any that poet has ever sung;
No knight of old, with spurs bedight
Could be to me a braver sight,
E'en though he went with plume and glove
To joust for the sake of his lady love.

And she—what maid of olden time,
Extolled in song or praised in rhyme,
Compares with her, whose form and face
Are perfect in their winsome grace?
They rode through the waning Summer's hours,
Where the sunlight sifted in golden showers
Through the woodland aisles in a solemn hush,
Through the firs and pine and hazel brush,
And down by the lessening river's brim
Where the sedge, with fingers long and slim,
Reached to the waters, clear and cool,
And dabbled in each shadowy pool.
Across their path the startled deer
Bounded away with a sudden fear;
The grouse, from the shade of the deepest wood,
Drummed and called to their mottled brood.
Again and again was softly heard
The tender fretting of some bird
That o'er her nest, in a shy alarm,
Hovered, to keep her young from harm;
The twittering quail to cover sped,
The silent rabbit as quickly fled.
They rode away through the pathways dim
To the redwood forest's farthest rim.

While the sun sank down in the Golden West
And rested awhile on the ocean's breast,
Into the forest, darkly dim—
I dreamed of them—she dreamed of him—
And he—not on the tented field,
Where there's on'y a life to take or yield—
Will this knight of mine his battle wage;
But amidst the strife of this wond'rous age,
Where swords are rusting, while gallant men
Reach nobler vict'ries by tongue or pen ;
Where the proudest destiny ever sought
Is to rule a king in the realm of thought.
And what of her?—O God above!
Keep her, and shield and crown with love;
The only thing of this world a part
That is worth the price of a woman's heart.
They have ridden away through the rosy light—
Ridden away from sound and sight;
Fairer than ever was writ or sung
To the clang of hoofs their laughter rung.
Into the future, dim and unknown,
They will go on—but I am alone,
Dreaming of them—from the world apart—
Their laughter echoes against my heart.

Sunset

THE evening's genius with his sword of flame
    Guards well the portal of the dying day;
His lance of light he strikes against the hills,
    Upon the highest breaks its glancing ray;
He marshals grandly on a crimson sea
His cloudship navy's golden argosy,
Whose flaunting banner in the sunset glow
Bids brave defiance to the dark'ning foe;
Who, swift advancing, o'er him softly flings
The purple shadow of the twilight's wings,
Till war's red flush before the night wind's breath
Fades out into the sullen gray of death,
And star-eyed night, prevailing all too soon,
Hangs out the silver sickle of the moon.

Good Friday

TO-DAY the Saviour died—suffered the Cruci-
  fied,
Yet could His failing eyes see the repentant's tear,
Saying: "In Paradise thou shalt with Me appear."
"Father, forgive!"   He prayed; such blessed
  words He said,
"They know not what they do." This in the face
  of death,
This for His enemies, asked with His latest breath.
Yet do His children now turn from His face and
  bow,
Not to this lowly one; down to strange gods beside;
And in their lust and pride, still is He crucified.

How long will they profane His pure and sacred
  name?
Placing His holy sign, His emblems so divine,
In midst of mockery, on each unhallowed shrine?

"I thirst!"--to each poor heart, struck by some
  poisoned dart,
Treading the narrow way—ready to faint and fall,

To the parched lips that cry, earth gives her bitter
    gall.
Oh, let us kneel to-day! kneel in the dust and
    pray,
Close to His bleeding feet; seeking our soul's
    relief,
In deep repentant grief—e'en like the dying thief.

Jesus, the "Prince of Peace," when shall the striv-
    ing cease?
Dark roll the waves of death; can we the current
    stem?
Seeing at last Thy face—touching Thy garment's
    hem?
Forgive each idle word Thy outraged ears have
    heard,
Each sinful act forgive; into Thy hands receive
At death our sorrowing souls, that they may live.
This day the Saviour died—suffered the Crucified;
Yet He, the suppliant, heard, and He could pity-
    ing see;
Saying: "In Paradise, to-day, thou shalt be
    with Me."

Christmas, 1890

WHEN, 'neath the stars of Bethlehem,
   The angels sang: "Good will to men,"
And "Peace on earth," a promise gave,
Since man was ransomed from the grave,
All earth, with sweet foreboding, smiled,
Because was born a homeless child.

A million spires point to the sky
   Where He, transfigured, took His flight,
Toward that great unsleeping Eye,
   Watching o'er death, and sin, and night.
For eighteen hundred years has been
   His triumph most devoutly sung,
O'er death, and sin, and suffering,
   In every clime—in every tongue.

Yet, while the organ grandly swells
   Within our great cathedral walls,
Chime answering chime of silvery bells,
   Upon the air of Christmas falls.

Fair women, decked in silk and lace,
Go warm and blest to softly pray,
And hasten to each sacred place
That gladly welcomes Christmas day.

Oh, Prince of Peace, who lived and died!
Oh, why upon this holy morn,
When sounds and scenes of reverence tell
This was the day that Thou wert born,
As from these temples of our pride
The happy worshipers have filed,
Why, cold and hungry, just outside,
Do we still find the homeless child?

A Golden Dream

IN MEMORY OF LEON.

———

WHERE the yellow Feather river
    Rolled its tide afar,
With its fruit, an orange laden,
    Grew at Bidwell's Bar.

There a little maid, one morning,
    Looking on the scene,
Tree and flower and fruit were mingled
    In a summer dream.

Steep the garden terrace—steeper
    Was the mountain side,
Where the scarlet trumpet creeper
    Trailed above the tide.

Not more scarlet was the blossom
    Than her dainty lips,
Like twin rose leaves, curved and folded,
    With exquisite tips.

And so soft and brown and changing
  Were her tender eyes,
Like a pool seen late in summer
  Where a shadow lies.

In her hands were tiger lilies,
  Gathered ere the sun
Had the time to kiss each chalice—
  Golden, every one.

As she gazed with gentle longing
  Through the lambent air,
A boy came running down the hillside,
  Crowned with tawny hair.

Blue his eyes—yes, blue as heaven,
  And his form and face
Promise bore of manly beauty,
  In their strength and grace.

O'er the garden wall he bounded,
  Plucking fruit and flower,
Tossed them to the little maiden
  In a fragrant shower.

Blushing, then, she thanked him sweetly,
　With a glad surprise
Dimpling all her smiling features,
　Shining from her eyes.

While a lady from the mansion,
　High above the tide,
" Leon, Leon," softly calling,
　Called him from her side.

*　*　*　*　*　*　*

As she bore her treasures homeward
　Over hill and stream,
All her pure young soul was lifted
　In a sunny dream.

Through the future rode to meet her,
　On a steed so rare,
A blue-eyed prince, in royal velvet,
　With long golden hair.

*　*　*　*　*　*　*

And so shrined in her fond mem'ry,
　Lived from day to day,
Crowned with curls of rippling splendor,
　Her own prince alway.

On life's sea, uneven, drifting,
  Each the other's face did see
Seldom; and death's fiat falling,
  Parted them eternally.

*   *   *   *   *   *   *

Not one orange tree, but thousands
  Grace the plains of Butte,
And like sands upon the sea shore
  Lies their golden fruit.

But one tree, where miners, delving,
  Left but seam and scar,
Crowning all the desolation
  In the past afar;

With its fruit and creamy blossoms,
  Each a separate star,
One no other tree can rival
  Grew at Bidwell's Bar.

And, alas! Time sees the passing
  Of all, good and fair—
Cold his heart—low in the grave mold
  Lies his golden hair.

"I Pass Her Grave"

HERE, to and fro—Time's wearied slave—
　I come and go, and pass her grave ;
A level lane—three roads divide,
Where I would fain oft pause beside,
I still pass by, on either side.

God help me!　As the whip of care
　Still urges on my lagging feet,
　No time to pray, no time to greet,
And save me ere I quite despair.
　Since she is lying with the dead,
　I have no place to lay my head,
And weep for all that I have borne.
I pass her grave, nor pause to mourn ;
　My heart alone stays with the dead.

To the Native Sons of the Golden West

TO the Native Sons of the Golden West,
  The genius of this bright century sings,
In a land where the kiss of the sun on her breast
  Gives life to a thousand beautiful things.

Where the golden orange and scarlet fire
  Of fragrant pomegranate blossoms shine ;
Where tropical beauty and northern balm
  Blend in the shadows of palm and pine.

To the Pioneer and the Native Son
  Give honor, O Land of the golden West!
One's work is over, but just begun
  For the other—for honor and fame the quest.

Happy the homes in a radiant land,
  And happy the maidens who will be blest,
In a country united in heart and hand,
  By the love of the sons of the Golden West.

To the Native Sons of the Golden West
    The Century's Genius prophetic sings—
Not alone of the past, but a future blest
    By a countless treasure of beautiful things.

September 9th, 1890.

"I Thirst"

" Darling, you may always know that I am as
constant as the sun."

THINK you the traveler on the desert waste,
    Dying of thirst, would still refuse to taste
When loving hands too gladly offered up
To the parched lips the overflowing cup?
This have I done; yet with beseeching hands,
Famished, my soul cries from life's desert sands.
As to the mirage returns the weary eyes,
Or as the lost look back to Paradise,
So to thy image, from this barren way,
My tortured spirit turns day after day.
Ere it is yielded, duty-worn and faint,
Uttering for thee its hopeless, last complaint,
Can it be sin, from this far waste of pain,
To crave some token of thy truth again?

"My Life is Devoted to Memories of You"

I SAILED beneath a burning sun,
By coral reefs and isles of balm,
Where orange groves and silvery palm
By faint spice winds were gently fanned,
Until I reached a tropic land.
And with three thousand miles between
The shores whereon two oceans fret,
I bravely said, " I will forget,"
And there beneath the Southern Cross
I crept out in the breathless night;
My heart was breaking, and the stars
Shone dimly on my fevered sight—
Ah! vain is change of time or place;
In heaven itself I see—thy face!

The Eclipse

AROUND a trackless waste of sky
   A dead world haunts this world of ours,
Upon whose pulseless breast no bird
May voice its joy among the flowers—
Whence life and love and all have fled
And left it silent, cold and dead.
The only thing that still seems bright,
The blessed sun's reflected light,
The tender radiance so serene
That falls in moonlight's silvery sheen.
As on my heart these shadowy thoughts
Had left the while their sombre trace,
A shadow from the weary world
Fell over Luna's ghost-like face.

Sonnet

———

YOU cannot come to me,
  But with this gift that God has given
I can reach out, o'er land and sea,
O'er barriers of earth and heaven,
And touch your heart exquisitely.
The bird caged with a golden wire
Sings not always for those who feed,
Supplying every grosser need ;
Above the tumult of her fate
She listens, and she hears her mate ;
She dreams a dream of vanished Springs,
She beats her wings, and sings, and sings—
The world says, "Sweetly sings"—but, oh !
You hear the undertone of woe.

Browning

—

HE died in Venice—citadel of songs,
　To which for ages all romance belongs;
At whose proud shrine the poet and the sage
Have left the offering of every age.

He died in Venice; but with dreaming eyes,
By the Rialto and the Bridge of Sighs;
And in and out a hundred water-ways,
For years he glided through the perfect days.

He died in Venice; but through all he dreamed
The golden sunshine of Italia streamed,
Where centered all those memories that endure
Around the home of Tasso and the Moor.

He died in Venice, but his work was done
Long years before his sands of life were run—
So ideal days he lived that did beseem
The closing visions of a poet's dream.

He died in Venice, where the lapping sea
Kept time to that diviner minstrelsy   [fraught
With which his gifted soul through time was
To live eternal in the world of thought.

But the worn garment that is left behind
They bear away to rest among its kind,
In that far land where, in the Abbey's shade,
Beside congenial dust, it will be laid.

A poet's love, a poet's life and death,
Blest from the earliest to his latest breath ;
But of all things that could his age befall,
To die in Venice seems the best of all.

fragment

MY heart has grown so heavy with the burden of
  its care,
That to Sorrow's gloomy portal I have fled and
  left no trace ;
But like moths from out the darknes to the light
  of thy loved face,
My thoughts go fluttering ever from the night of
  my despair.

Love's Magic Seal

OFT have I smiled, when in youth's halcyon time,
  I heard in song, or read in deathless rhyme,
How gallant knights, bedight in plume and glove,
Had met and fought, and gladly died for love.
How ladies, too, and maidens wondrous fair,
Had wept, and pined, and died in love's despair;
How Guinivere her crown and fame forgot,
And sweet Elaine had died for Launcelot;
How Cleopatra, on the storied Nile,
Did Antony from all the world beguile;
How brave Colonna mourned beside the sea
Her worshiped lord, till death had set her free;
How Abelard the cloister vainly sought,
And saintly Heloise her vows forgot.
Oft then I smiled; for love, in that bright hour,
Seemed to my fancy but a boasted power;
But now these things, prefiguring my fate,
  But faintly symbol all I know and feel;
This ardent passion, time cannot abate,
  Since on my soul, love set his magic seal.

Ode to Progress

PRIZE POEM

Awarded the gold medal by the Agricultural Association of Lake and Mendocino
Counties, 1887.

GENIUS of this grand century, and guardian of
    the free,
Who can a tribute worthily bring from our hearts
    to thee?
When, 'neath the Star of Bethlehem, angels sang
    that blessed morn,
"Peace on earth, good will to all men," Progress,
    thou wert also born.
The ages past had never known thee, for man un-
    just oppressed
His fellow man; who, suffering, saw might as right
    confessed.
Ask Egypt's hordes, who toiled as helpless slaves
To build her kings imperishable graves;
Or Grecian art, that on each heathen fane
Left us the dower of some immortal name;
Or Rome's imperial grandeur crumbling down,
If it was Progress marked their great renown.

No! since the world and all its works began,
Have Art and Science been the slaves of man ;
Degraded oft, ignoble scopes to fill,
To suit the vagaries of the human will.
So Freedom's smile o'er Superstition's horde
Accomplished more than power of fire and sword;
While Christian liberty, o'er land and sea,
Enlightens all, and makes the poorest free ;
And things that were but dreams to Greece and
   Rome,
With us to grand realities have grown.
A homeless child so touched the human soul,
He made the world akin—one wondrous whole.
His story echoes down the aisles of time,
In every language told by tongues sublime ;
Nor will it cease till every land has heard
The precious promise of His sacred word,
That truth and justice shall prevail alone—
Where they are not, Progress, thou art not
   known.

"Miles Are Between Us"

MILES are between us, and the relentless night
   Follows the sullen day in sombre flight;
Above the pine-woods in the distant west
The clouds lie piled, a burden of unrest.
I know you love me, but the chains that hold
Were forged by destiny—relentless—cold;
They keep me from you, like a serpent's fold.
But I cast all from me, that my fate has wrought,
And hasten to you in my anguished thought.
Thank God! no other holds the place I crave
On earth, or hidden in the solemn grave
No woman rivals me; whate'er has been
In this impassioned dream, I only sin.
I cannot tell you, hero of my heart,
How much I love you when so far apart.
The world's best teaching holds us—honor, pride—
But in a dream, unspeaking, by your side,
I still may follow, safe from sound and sight,
While the relentless day closes in sullen night.

June

BETWEEN the roses of the May
　　Looks out the radiant face of June;
Blushing, she seems afraid to cross
　　The threshold of the Spring so soon;
While my heart echoes, beat for beat,
The tread of her reluctant feet.

Passionate languor in her eyes,
　　The kiss of Summer on her mouth—
I love her harmony of birds—
　　I love her soft winds of the South—
Her cumulus clouds that grandly rise
Across the sunlight of her skies.

A lily with its laughing lips
　　Opes as she smiles—a star-like shine
Thrills me from heart to finger-tips
　　With fragrance of the jessamine;
A dove her gentle note prolongs,
Answering the last late robin's songs.

As here I fondly weave my dreams,
　　While waiting—face to face with June—
Of you, my darling—beautiful
　　As bird-song, blossom and perfume—
Lulled on the Summer's slumberous breast,
I dream, and know that I am blest.

Sonnet

———

WE are so far apart—even from ocean to ocean—
  As a nun would tell her beads, only with more
    devotion,
Counting the days when we met,
As the chain slips over my fingers,
Over each thought of you my heart caressingly
  lingers.
The long, bright lance of the sun,
Reaching away from the sunset,
Touches my hair and eyes,
And the lips you kissed, when you told me,
Constant you'd always be while the sun in his
  shining should hold me.
The heart and the lips you love, grow warm his
  red rays under.
Constant I know you are, though we are so far
  asunder.
God bless and keep you so on the shore of another
  ocean—
As a nun her beads, the hours I tell, only with
  more devotion.

"No Babes In Arms"

A SATIRE

Suggested by seeing the above notice at the entrance to one of our fashionable theatres.

———

WHILE Fashion trips within the door
   That Thespis opens wide before her,
Pleasure and Vice, and many more,
   Beside their goddess quickly enter,
Folly comes in, and Crime, her brother—
   All children of the same vile mother;
The courtesan, with painted charms—
But listen, not "the babe in arms."

For Innocence there is no place
   In all this grand and brilliant throng;
'Tis well, for on its modest face
   Blushes must burn for scene and song;
Or, if unconscious, still its cries
   Might through the tearful silence steal,
Marring the sense of ears and eyes
   That drink the rantings of Camille.

Camille, sin-stamped, her life of crime
   Can never touch an honest heart,

E'en painted by the fingers fine
   Of sentiment and finished art,
Forgive all like her, and wish them good,
But ask not true, pure womanhood
To shed the sympathetic tear
Over her guilty, weak career.

     *   *   *   *   *

Over the rich man's palace gate
   Those words might well be placed quite often,
When nothing can his craving sate,
   His greed for power, and pride of station.
Some prince of style, with endless means,
   Whose social traits—a strange transition
From when he lived on "pork and beans"—
   Now swell with limitless ambition.

His wife, in fashion's trappings decked,
   Now leads a band of kindred spirits,
Of whom she is the "great elect,"
   To "kettledrums" and other places;
Forgetting how, in earlier times,
She once scoured kettles in the mines
Before she hoisted o'er her charms
The motto of "No babes in arms."

Her fragile health admits no more
   The cares that earnest woman busy;
Though grand receptions by the score
   Cannot fatigue, nor dancing weary.
"A babe so breaks a mother's rest!"
As all her thousand friends attest,
While gossiping their usual way
Of husbands who are apt to stray,

And have a liking for their club,
   Where everybody smokes and swaggers,
While telling cronies where's the rub
   In politics and other matters.
A bad state of affairs at best,
   For husbands, wives, and all the rest.

No sleep at Nature's fittest time—
   The night filled with unholy revel.
What wonder that their faces wear
   Too oft the look of heartless devils?
And men who could have loved, at rest,
A baby on a mother's breast—
To view with interest are agog
A "thing" that pets a poodle-dog.
    *   *   *   *   *

The eyes of faith have looked beyond
   This life, that even at its best
Is filled with care and pain untold—
   Its triumphs filled with strange unrest,
And pictured an existence grand
And glorious in an unknown land,
Where all that pure in heart have been
As little children enter in.

While over all the hopeless dead,
   Entering at last the gates of doom,
That sentence unrevoked and dread,
   God's fiat traces in the gloom,
To meet and blast despairing eyes
That turn away from Paradise
And read above Hell's wild alarms:
"There enter here no babes in arms."

fragment

[IN AN ALBUM.]

I WILL not wish you gold, or love, or fame—
   Too many sins, committed in their name,
Sweep through the ages, and with dark surprise
Their annals blast the light of artless eyes.
Virtue alone can bless and crown your youth,
Therefore I consecrate its days to truth.

To the University of California

ECCA of my ~~lost~~ youth,
　Between thy shrine and my sad heart,
The years with pallid faces stand
　And hold us far apart.

I reached aspiring hands
　Hung'ring toward thy "mount of light;"
God filled them, measuring not my plans—
　He doeth all things right.

His tasks appointed well,
　To idle heart-break not allied,
Gave nature as my "Alma Mater"
　And duty for my guide.

But echoes of thy fame
　Waft by on wings of memory,
And day by day my constant thoughts
　Like prilgrims go to thee.

Death of General Grant

A MONODY

READ BY THE AUTHOR AT THE MEMORIAL EXERCISES AT UKIAH,
MENDOCINO COUNTY, CALIFORNIA, AUGUST 8TH, 1885.

———

WHO has not stood within the chilling gloom
   Where some bright pathway ended in the
      tomb,
And from its portal could no longer trace
A future—blank, for want of one loved face
Then, dazed and broken, blindly faltering back,
Resumed the round of life's repellent track ?
What family circle has not broken been
By this decree, provoked by man's first sin?
This awful mystery; whose fingers cold
Can touch impartially the young or old,
Point out the fairest for the fatal dart,
And still the beating of the noblest heart.
No pride of station and no boast of power
Prolongs a life for even one short hour.
The cottager or claimant of a throne,
On God's great mercy both depend alone;

No other power, at last, endures to save,
And all distinctions level in the grave.
Toil's implement—the monarch's royal crown,
At that dark threshold are alike laid down.
We come as beggars from the Master's hand,
And at life's close, we still as suppliants stand—
Oh! may His mercy, like a mantle, fall
At that dread hour, in charity, on all.
What, though our burdens be of pain and care,
So great they seem, more than the heart can bear;
Be patient still, we all will lay them soon
Down by the portals of the quiet tomb;
And in the silence of that awful shade,
How many a fault to nothingness will fade!
The hoarded treasures of the countless years
Have been resigned before that shrine of tears.
For there, each heart has said a last "good-bye,"
And broken there is every earthly tie—
And when we hold the wreaths that triumph gave,
We all turn back to lay them on some grave.

*   *   *   *   *   *   *   *   *

What meed of praise—what tribute shall we pay
To him the nation meets to mourn to-day?

Who danger's gauntlet oft in safety ran ;
Who lived a hero, but to die a man.
He was but human—but his faults were few ;
His life was honest, and his purpose true.
Blame not that noble one, that fortune led
His feet where war had made the pathway red—
His country called ; he did her grief assuage,
And saved America her heritage.
Where wrong has been, alone, God knoweth best,
And there alone His punishment will rest.
But no just thought confuses now with him
That awful scourging of a people's sin.
Over his coffin, sorrowing to-day,
Bow'd are the vet'rans of the blue and gray.
Over his grave, unworthy strife will cease,
And North and South clasp hands in lasting peace.
The flag, whose honor he has saved, hangs low ;
And all the land is draped in signs of woe ;
And many a cheek with honest tears is wet,
Now, that at last his star of life is set.
But though the flowers we bring be doomed to fade,
And loving hands that weave them shall be laid
To moulder back into the common clay,
Forgotten—like the tributes of this day—

He leaves one thing, that will not be forgot,
To live immortal in the people's thought.
When liberty, enlightening the world,
All false usurpers from their thrones has hurled;
When creeds no more perplex fanatic fools,
Who live by rote, and worship God by rules;
When parties die—and prejudice is dead—
And ignorance—and in their narrow stead,
A people live, by truth and reason led—
A Christian people o'er the whole earth spread—
Then will the greatness of this man be known;
Though back to dust the monumental stone
Has crumbled, his memory will shine
Throughout the ages of all coming time.
So fear not now, within the Nation's sight,
This glorious epitaph of him to write:
He leaves, emblazoned on the scroll of fame,
The matchless splendor of a deathless name.

"I Do Begrudge To Time"

I DO begrudge to time this lip's fond red,
    This heart's warm pulse, that beat with hope
      and truth
Through all the years, while lingered yet my
    youth,
By love's assurance most divinely fed.
Into the face of pain I bravely looked,
Nor shrank before the horrid face of death.
While I could hope to meet thy constant eyes,
For me life's desert seemed a paradise.
But O my darling! I am sad to-night;
Upon the edge of duty and of care
The finer fabrics of my life are worn;
My ardent being feels a strange despair—
That time prevails; and e'en for thy dear sake,
The heart that was so brave will surely break.

To a Charming Portrait of a Gypsy Maiden

Lines dedicated to the hard-working and poorly-paid artists of California.

———

MY pretty little Gypsy, you've caused me bitter
    woe ;
But how, my little Gypsy, no man shall ever know.
For I shall never tell it, and you will never speak,
And so, between the two of us, the secret we will
    keep.

Your eyes are dark and solemn, beneath each
    raven tress,
As though you sought to question the cause of
    my distress ;
And so, although you've brought me a grief I
    shall not name,
I like to sit and watch you, and I love you all the
    same.

You have never told my fortune, but you comfort
    and you bless,
For your eyes, with tender glances, are like a
    mute caress,
As with fawn-like grace and freedom you stand
    and look at me,
Your lovely arm entwining the sturdy greenwood
    tree.

And I thank a kindly Providence that in this age
  of greed,
When every selfish worldling makes gain his only
  creed,
There are a few brave spirits who, in the sordid
  strife,
Catch and hold, with pen or pencil, the lovelier
  things of life.

A bit of charming landscape, an eye alight with
  love—
A thought that inspiration has sought and found,
  above
The plane, where many thousands toil and strive
  till life has flown,
To build up, for the thankless, their piles of brick
  and stone.

The hand whose cunning caught you, from fancy
  or from fact,
Whose brush on canvas fixed you, with genius and
  with tact,
My gratitude shall follow along Time's checkered
  flight,
For to me my little Gypsy will bring life-long
  delight.

"The Gladdest Heart"

———

THE gladdest heart in all the world is mine—
   And yet, like showers that fall aslant the shine
Of April suns, and, in a tearful way,
Deny the radiant splendor of the day,
This sobbing breath—these tears upon my cheek,
Give sad denial to the words I speak.
For in the years betwixt this and the grave,
And that long rest its solemn silence brings,
While shines for us the blest and constant sun,
Through Autumn's sere and flower-encircled
   Springs,
There waits no day that we may call our own
Upon this sin-cursed earth—the slave of time—
When I may answer you and tell you why
The gladdest heart in all the world is mine.

Sacramento

IN the moonlight, o'er the sidewalk, long the
    shadows fall,
And trace so restlessly their shape upon the con-
    vent wall;
While my heart, with all its longing to that city
    far and dim,
Turns to-night, despite of distance—is again with
    him.

And upon his face I see the shadow of the years,
As he might, upon my own, read the traces of
    my tears—
And still nearer than the nearest I am with him in
    my thought;
Does my spirit seek his presence, wild with yearn-
    ing, thus unsought?

No; and so it reaches, in the night so sweet and
    still,
Over rock and plain and meadow, o'er valley
    land and hill,

Over all the years of hunger, for the blessing of
  his smile,
And unspeaking lingers near his side a little while.

Once, the tide of life all thrilling, in a Summer's
  night,
Clasped a moment in his arms, I touched the
  borders of delight ;
But I turned, my being shaken, and with faltering,
  aimless feet,
Fled for years the love forbidden, still so strangely
  sweet.

And those waves of feeling, breaking through the
  cruel years,
Leave my heart a hopeless wreck, beneath the
  current of my tears ;
Yet it turns with all its yearning to that city, far
  and dim,
And to-night, all else forgetting, is again with him.

Ante Mortem

WHEN this strange garment that my soul has
    worn
  Has burned away beneath the fitful flashes
Of that wild fever that no cure has known,
  Until the heart consumes to coldest ashes
"Life's fitful fever," burning with such loss
  Of thought and feeling—earth's diviner treasure,
So many precious things among the dross,
  Their value would a life-time take to measure.

When "dust to dust" a strange voice softly says,
  And sadly drop the valley clods above me,
While telling o'er the events of my days,
  Amid the tears of those who think they love me;
If they could know the seeming endless pain
  That I had passed beyond—and died,
They would not, surely, wish me back again,
  Where all that's Christ-like still is crucified.

That priceless debt the world cannot repay—
  A child's lost faith in all its vain assurance,

The hope that turns toward a brighter day,
  Through months of toil, and patience, and en-
    durance.
This is the sum, too oft, through changing years,
  Of sacrifice no words may fitly tell;
And so, despite the most regretful tears,
  We sleep, "after life's fitful fever," well.

I have so suffered—thus a glad relief
  Seems possible; and now, as Time is fleeting,
I look where death stands, just beyond my grief,
  And know that there no pulse of pain is beating;
Where sin, ingratitude, and pride and lust,
  That have so marred the frail thing I am wearing,
Lying beside that poor handful of dust,
  Are left at last, while I go on uncaring.

———

www.ingramcontent.com/pod-product-compliance
Lightning Source LLC
Chambersburg PA
CBHW021633270326
41931CB00008B/999